Also by Philip Fried

MUTUAL TRESPASSES
(Ion, 1988)

QUANTUM GENESIS
(Zohar, 1997)

BIG MEN SPEAKING TO LITTLE MEN
(Salmon, 2006)

COHORT
(Salmon, 2009)

EARLY/LATE: NEW AND SELECTED POEMS
(Salmon, 2011)

INTERROGATING WATER AND OTHER POEMS
(Salmon, 2014)

FOUR AMERICAN POETS
Anthony Costello, Editor of the anthology
(The High Window, 2016)

ACQUAINTED WITH THE NIGHT
(Rizzoli, 1997) (With Lynn Saville), Editor

salmonpoetry

Squaring the Circle
PHILIP FRIED

Published in 2017 by
Salmon Poetry
Cliffs of Moher, County Clare, Ireland
Website: www.salmonpoetry.com
Email: info@salmonpoetry.com

Copyright © Philip Fried, 2017

ISBN 978-1-910669-74-7

All rights reserved. No part of this publication may be reproduced or transmitted in any form or by any means, electronic or mechanical, including photography, recording, or any information storage or retrieval system, without permission in writing from the publisher. The book is sold subject to the condition that it shall not, by way of trade or otherwise, be lent, resold or otherwise circulated without the publisher's prior consent in any form of binding or cover other than that in which it is published and without a similar condition, including this condition, being imposed on the subsequent purchaser.

COVER PHOTOGRAPHY: *Lynn Saville*
COVER DESIGN & BOOK TYPESETTING: *Siobhán Hutson*
Printed in Ireland by Sprint Print

To my mother,
Mollie Ellen Fried (1921–2015),
in loving memory
blessèd are the troublemakers
who hunger and thirst after justice

Acknowledgements

Thanks are due to the editors of the following journals and anthologies, where these poems will appear or have appeared, sometimes in earlier versions:

AGNI: "The Quantum Mechanics of Everyday Life"; *Barrow Street*: "Arrival"; "God Says"; *Caveat Lector*: "Hop on, Hop off"; "Entanglement"; *Even The Daybreak: 35 Years of Salmon Poetry* Anthology: "Late in the Game"; *The High Window*: "Thirteen Ways of Looking at a Paper Clip"; *Jewish Currents*: "Misdirection": *The Lampeter Review*: "Drone"; "Ballyhoo"; "Hullabaloo"; *Literal Latte*: "Gadget" (as "Contraptions"); *Notre Dame Review*: "God, the Busker"; "God as Float"; *Offcourse*: "Guided Meditation in the People's House"; "Package Insert" (as "Duellum [du 'el lum]: Uses, Side Effects, and Contra-indications"); "Maniac I"; *Plume*: "Prequel"; *Plume Anthology*, Volume 3: "Cloud of Knowing"; *Poet Lore*: "In Triplicate"; *Poetry*: "Squaring the Circle"; *Poetry Quarterly*: "Midrash on Genesis"; *The Poetry Review*: "Irrational, Imaginary" (as "Irrationals"); "The Full Treatment"; *Saint Ann's Review*: "Event/Horizon"; "Golden Rule"; *Skidrow Penthouse*: "Pre-Post-Apocalyptic Jump-Rope"; "Take the Memory Quiz"; *Warscapes*: "What Happened After the End?"; *The Warwick Review*: "Powers of 10"; "God, the Younger."

"Squaring the Circle" was featured on the *Poetry Daily* website, July 22, 2014.

I would like to express my gratitude to Mark Sullivan and D. Nurkse for their editorial advice. I am also deeply grateful to Jessie Lendennie, my publisher, for her unstinting support; to Siobhán Hutson for her wonderful book designs; and to Lynn, for everything.

Contents

Powers of 10

Powers of 10	10
The Game of Skully	11
We Rented	12
Irrational, Imaginary	13
God, the Younger	14
X is the Solution	15
Gadget	16
God, the Elder	17
Squaring the Circle	18
Late in the Game	19
Midrash on Genesis	20
The Full Treatment	21
Cloud of Knowing	22
PTSD	23
Prequel	24
God as Float	26
Arrival	27
God Says …	28
Fore- and Aftershocks	29
In Triplicate	30
God, the Busker	31

The Quantum Mechanics of Everyday Life

Hallucination	33
The Quantum Mechanics of Everyday Life	34
Event/Horizon	35
SOK, WHAP …	36
"Knee on concrete, …"	37
Pilot Episode, October, 1962	38
Happy Hour	39
Hop on, Hop off	40
Entanglement	41

Cutting Edge

"I Dreamt That I Dwelt in Marble Halls"	44
Golden Rule	45
Thirteen Ways of Looking at a Paper Clip	46
"We are such stuff ..."	49
"no ideas but in things ..."	50
Recipes.gov	51
Cutting-Edge Agronomy	53
Posterity Posse	54
Drone	56
Take the Memory Quiz	57
Interrogating *Stress*	58
Emblems	59
"We, therefore ..."	60
Pre-Post-Apocalyptic Jump-Rope	61
What Happened After the End?	62

The World's Big Show

Package Insert	65
Guided Meditation in the People's House	67
MANIAC I	69
Please Listen Carefully	70
Yoga for Leaders and Others	71
Striking a Tone, with Overtones	73
Misdirection	74
Whose Advice Was Crucial in Your Quest for Stardom?	75
Flagony Column: Advice from a Vexillologist	76
Summer's End	78
Wanted	79
Coulrophobia	81
Ballyhoo	83
Hullabaloo	84

Powers of 10

Powers of 10

Numbers are given to us in the air we breathe—
Parents are two; sister, one more than one—
And decimals, a survival kit, by our teacher,
Strips of cardboard, bundled in rubberbands:

In a world no longer pointless, powers of ten.
At the age of 5, one of us loses a nickel
Never to be recovered, but reimbursed
In the newly-minted notion that any nickel's

Good for five pennies, stripped of sentiment.
Names are the pledge that each one of us counts
For something precious, invaluable, and nameless.
But numbers are given to us in the air we breathe.

Factories are manufacturing many items
For us, but the smoke from their chimneys is the shifting
Shape of namelessness, a bitter odor.
We are still living, lacking this or that,

In a post-war world of abundance and wonder.
Pity poor grandmother and grandfather,
Who have survived, time's refugees, with just
One or two things—copper tray, samovar.

Their knowledge is vast and vague, their years nearly countless.
Early on, I'm taught to believe in a God who is One,
Whose Number is given to us before the air,
The names, the Word or the void that is not even shapeless …

The Game of Skully

When was the parallel postulate set aside
So that lines, by now far out in space, are curving
Toward each other or away, and all
This time, aligning tanks and tin battalions
Or intent above the chalk-ruled skully court
(The playground pavement gnawing on my knee),
To flick a bottle cap, I am a killer
Euclidean in a non-Euclidean world,

Making a circuit of the trapezoids
Surrounding square 13, the "skull," intoning
The murderous mantra, earning my asphalt degree,
And a trillion of me could fit on a mica fleck
In the Demiurge's court, while the axiom "God"
Asserts that the playground is curved, unbounded, and good?

We Rented

We rented rooms in data's metropolis,
paying each month to live statistically free,
subject only to the rates for life
expectancy, suicide, morbidity,
guided by provisos for the average
family size, number of cars, and income,
and signaling when we crossed any median.

Adorning bodies with vulgar signs and symbols
was a nasty habit of bikers and screwloose sailors,
but we liked intoning numbers from the news,
a form of aural tattoo: the body count,
the market uptick, and the missile countdown.

At 13 you were no longer a boy, the holy
scroll of childhood memory wrapped in ribbons,
a Torah, now unwrapped, unrolled, a foreign
tongue to be chanted back to relatives.

The One God was wearing bright white gloves,
signaling from the top of the Tower of Babel,
like a tic-tac man, the shifting prices and odds.

Irrational, Imaginary

In math in the back of the room and partially
Hidden by Jimmy Dulnik's prominent skull,
I was day-dreaming of mom and dad as two
Integers whose ratio could not fully
Express me, I who was not famous like Pi,
Not yet anyway, but a garden variety square
Root of, take your pick, 3, 5, or 11,

And so could go on and on and on, and was God,

I wondered, Imaginary—"By accepting,
Class, that *i* exists, we can solve things"—pacing
Backward, just a pair of giant footsteps,
Through the vacant garden, and a muttering—
"Square root of a minus, the subversive *i*"—
  (All things arising there from His absent mind)
As pollen perpetually falls through the no-air?

God, the Younger

Open the brackets of the empty set ...

God sneaked into the master closet, to fit
His boy's foot into someone's larger shoes—
A larger people will need a bigger God,
He reasoned, but, for now, it's a bit wobbly.

Perched on a throne of chair and telephone books
At the dressing table, beneath bright burning suns,
And magnified in the mirror, God affixes
A creator's mighty beard with spirit gum.

After a dull and rainy day in heaven,
The picture window breaks out in a rash of speckles,
Marks that mean nothing, but he imagines one smudge
Is the island that will grant him courage and love.

Not until high school would he learn about sets
From his teacher E. Integer, a checkers whiz.
They contained all or nothing, and everything
In-between, but the coolest one was named *empty*

Or *null*, a word pronounced with the disdain
And pride that made a rigorous theory viable.
What power in None, the cape that adorned your utter
Absence. What could he not create from under

That cloak when he grew up ... Close brackets.

X is the Solution

> *Glove box: a sealed protectively lined compartment having holes to which are attached gloves for use in handling especially dangerous materials inside the compartment.*
> —Merriam-Webster Dictionary

Glove box, fit for a deity,
Absolutely insulating.
Disposable Neoprene gloves, part
Polymer—same molecules used
In rocket fuels—part algebra.
X is the solution, not
The unknown, in a set-up with rapid
Access doors. Multiple containment
Chambers with constant negative pressure.
Isolates operator from toxic
Environment. Dual-side viewing
Windows reveal civilizations
Teeter-tottering as fumes
Are sucked up into chamber ceiling.
Operator safely handles
Plutonium, deer ticks, chicken pox, peoples.
Numbers guaranteed to replace
Faces of every type of victim
In this ventilated mini-verse.

Gadget

Seduced by the billiard-ball physics of Rube Goldberg,
God became addicted to convoluted

Contraptions for accomplishing simple tasks,
Like the self-operating napkin, ungainly

Gizmo or gadget concocted from skyrocket, pail,
Soup spoon, and parrot, inspiring Him to create

A Galileo that would knock Aristotle's
Head against Plato's, activating a shout

Eureka! as feathers tumbled out of the sky
Like lead, a mass of them depressing a lever

That with a *whirr* released a pendulum
To swing from the leaning tower toward Mrs. Laufer's

Class and trigger a siren impelling us
To duck and cover, hands over eyes, averting

Our faces from the windows, protecting our sight
From the fireball that would soon be melting the glass.

God, the Elder

Latin of course existed from the beginning,
Almost coeval with Him.... *A priori*,
He loves the authoritative roll of a phrase,
Reminisces about the rigor of forfeiture,

The thrill of designating the losing party,
Detention, irrevocable orders of seizure.
O for primeval times, when the law showed claw
And a *writ of ne exeat* really had bite!

Now there are unzipped robes, polyester rulings,
Trials simulcast with play-by-play
Analysis, and a continual
Appeal to Him in his total absence, place

Your hand on these worn and red-edged words, and swear
(Atheists can merely claim to be moral)!
While He Himself is serving an infinite sentence
In Heaven's minimum security prison,

Day-dreaming He's back at the start of it all, proclaiming
Let there be darkness, then *fiat lux!* Alas,
He lacks the precedents, but preserves the Latin,
Like down in a pillow composed of feathers plucked

From the wings of Justice, that rare, endangered bird,
Dispatched by the 12-gauge judgment of Authority,
And retrieved by the eager pack of lawyers and bailiffs—
All to bear up, and give rest to, His Legal Brain.

Ipso facto one could fall asleep
In a condition of postprandial bliss,
Issuing a summons, deciding a claim,
Separating the goats from the sheep, the sheep ...

Squaring the Circle

It's a little-known fact that God's headgear—
A magician's collapsible silk top hat,
When viewed from Earth, from the bottom up—
Is, *sub specie aeternitatis*,

A pluperfect halo, both circle and square,
And a premonition of this truth
Spurred on an ancient philosopher,
Anaxagoras, to make numerous vain

Attempts to approximate the circle
Of his concerns with the square of the cell
He was jailed in for impiety.
Doomed calculations which God acknowledged

By doffing then pancaking his topper.
He was still bareheaded millennia later,
When he learned of von Lindemann's proof that Pi
Is not the root of a polynomial

With rational coefficients, hence
Squaring the circle's impossible.
God un-collapsed, re-donned his hat!
But—it was 1882,

Progress was a juggernaut
And the public had no patience for "proof."
From below, God's gesture looked like a signal
For all hat- and cap-wearing men,

Proper in their headgear, for nations,
Well-stocked with helmets for delicate brain-work,
To take up "the compass and straightedge"
And prepare for a singular all-out attack

On this seductive conundrum, so men
Enlisted en masse in Geometry's army,
Tossing up and away all hats
Of cloth, opaque haloes, hurray!

Late in the Game

In heaven's bleachers, it's the 7th-inning
Stretch. God and Gödel, standing side by side,
Cap on head, Bible and scorecard on seat,
Are gazing down at the green in America's soul.

Want a dog and a tall cold one? asks God.
Thanks, no, Gödel demurs, *I never indulge.*
I am, I admit, sparing in what I eat.
But, as I was saying, the incompleteness theorem
"Knocked the legs out from under," is that the idiom?,
Russell and Whitehead's quest for an unbroken, logical
Basis for mathematics.
                      Just what I did
To the snake, says God. *That slithery hissing devil,*
That terrorist ...
              By the way, I proved you exist,
Ontologically, by using an ultrafilter,
Together with a modal plenitude principle.
—Awesome!
          But I've discovered a logical flaw
In the Constitution, an inner contradiction
That could make a dictatorship legal.
                              You're a good citizen,
On earth as in heaven. Can't give you a Halo Dog?
—It's in the section about executive power.
You see, Mr. God, or President? ...
                              Just then,
The Seraphim finish their cover, to loud acclaim,
Of "God Bless America," the boisterous crowd
Of the blessed, re-seated, is stirring, and He is purring,
That's ok, kid, but let's get back to the game.

Midrash on Genesis

Proper in his white coat, God will never
Violate the doctor-patient privilege
And divulge what happened in the timeless time

Before time, but imagine the feats of memory
In this pre-digital, pre-vellum Limbo,
Not to mention the infinite interview rooms

In what we might call a medical caravansary,
But which itself could fit in a dust mote.
Even for Him the task of gaining unanimous

Consent was daunting, so He must have outsourced
Some of the process to Creation Associates.
And though each session, and these were countless, took less

Than an instant, there was time enough for every
Formidable resistance to present.
Take the sparrow, parabolic bird,

And so a case God handled himself. It was spec'd
As a stubby, small, strong-beaked, brown-gray, seed-eater,
For whom, if it consented to exist

And assumed all risks, He pledged a watchfulness.
But first He had to cure the incipient sparrow's
Bird-of-paradise urge for rainbow plumage

And a rainforest life, rich in polygamy.
Would you rather be taken for granted, or hunted
For skin and feathers, threatened with habitat loss?

Relenting, the passerine signed the Existence Agreement,
Renouncing all claims to be paradisaeidae
By dabbing a talon in ink, making its mark.

Don't even think of asking Him how much
Downtime, how many a sanity break He took
In this pre-prelude. Creation was a huge headache.

The Full Treatment

Algebrista y Sangrador

Barbering, bonesetting, bloodletting, it's all
In the equation, the unknown revealed, the patient
Healed, as proclaimed by the helical red-and-white pole,
Sign of a site of bandages and blood,
Where stubble's harvested, the left sideburn
Leveled with the right, a bubo lanced,
A famine lamented, the whispers of new belief
Drowned out by the slap of the blade on a leather strop,
As the neck's interrogated in a close
Shave, accenting the trim and pointy beard,
Blood's drawn in quantity from the crook of the arm,
Hair cut short and bobbed for a market economy,
Molar extracted, hernia repaired,
No amputation necessary, as yet,
Bone broken by heresy reset, to knit
Almost smooth and intact, and God is groomed
Cured, powdered, sprinkled with eau de cologne, back-slapped
And sent out to succeed in a new era.

Cloud of Knowing

God's a committed statistician,
An acolyte of decision science,
Intent on minimizing risk,
Constantly seeking optimization,
Cognizant of each fallen sparrow,
The regrettable fact of collateral damage,
But figuring outcomes for the flock.

With his green plastic gambler's visor—
A nod to nostalgia's not amiss,
A wink at the old theory of forms—
In a room as far from Plato's cave
As warmer-toned fluorescence can take him,
Cocooned by arrays of supercomputers
Galloping at an exaflop rate,
With a single index finger, he inputs
Commands for drones named for archangels.

Anyway, a cave's down below
Somewhere, while he's in a floating, nowhere
Cloud …
        Often, he'll don a big pair of headphones
To tune in on, and monitor,
The earthly chatter from everywhere.

PTSD

The one great shock of having been
God in the age-old recent wars
When with flood and fire he razed
The cities of the plain, the tower
Of Babel ... The little aftershocks ...

He decreed a people's destiny,
Shepherding their leaders and prophets.
Now the least suburban pothole
Triggers a spasm of strategizing,
And raking and burning leaf-litter

Summons the fearful bursts of flame
Consuming and not consuming the bush.
The men he commanded, ordaining the law,
The years in the desert wilderness,
Companionship and wild speculation

Like a foretaste of milk and honey—
Replaced by the nod in the supermarket.
The mission, stunted, is now the chore.
The hierarchy of the heavens—
Rank on rank of angels in place,

Downward toward earth, their eyes upward—
Morphed to the amorphous family,
With rooms that are booby-trapped with toys,
Intimate, explosive demands.
Sacred anger to irritability.

He lets the TV dream for him,
A confabulation of pixels, leans back,
His omniscient eye scanning each actor
In the sit-com, but winces a bit
With every burst of canned laughter.

Prequel

Who hath put wisdom in the inward parts?
   —Book of Job

Take a seat. All you need to know is, I am
The DA, judge, and jury in one, a justice
System. I investigate even nano-whispers
Of complaint about providing prey to raptors,
And I'll say, though it hardly needs to be said, I'm invested
With breathtaking powers, etc.

Why did you flee into the wilderness
Of your cerebrum? Nevermind. Every obscure
Clearing can be accessed by divine
Megaphone and floodlit by the Logos.
How did we track you? I hear it all, every bit
Of the planet's chatter. News and newsleaks, sexting,
Conspiracies, the wind colluding with leaves.
I am sui generis and omni-aural
As well as omniscient and omnipotent.

And you've become a person of interest, a notable.
Right to remain silent? We're not a procedural!
Of course. You can make *more* than one call. Reach out.
But would even a mafia mouthpiece dare to plead
For a human speck in the Court of the Absolute?

Where were you at the time of the classified
Incident? Don't tell me you were just doodling
With syntax. You devised a silent soliloquy
Of feeble, sulky dissent. Your speech, from a tangle
Of neurons, flowered into orchids like *justice*,
Or nettles like *motherfucker*. But the mind
Is a leased wilderness, whose excitable cells
Can be tapped.

          Here's the plea deal: you'll act as my witness,
Rehearse the authorized narrative, rescind
Your complaint, endorse my initiative to feed
The raptor, and bow to my superior terror.
I want to know everything I already know.
Stand up. Begin with the voice from the whirlwind …

God as Float

Have I been Disneyfied? God wonders,
Awakening in the cold pre-dawn
As a float awaiting the parade
That might or might not begin. Suspended
By pulleys, he realizes he's a leviathan
Mishmash of tools and industrial rubbish

And dreams of the upcoming rituals:
As I pass through crowds, a parade of one,
Children will leap at me, trying to snatch
A rake, green tube, or backhoe bucket
From my assemblage—to them, a giant
Jungle gym that bristles with prizes.

Adults will venture mental jumps
By first identifying each item
Of their collective life that shapes
Me—hammer, hardhat, battery,
Wire, wheelbarrow, tire, fan—
Before they make more speculative leaps

With questions of form and augury.
Is it a dragon or an explosion,
A phoenix or a porcupine-cloud?
Does it bode well or ill? And I'll want
To cry out, *I'm what hovers above
Your heart's abandoned construction site.*

Arrival

When the visitor from oblivion deplaned,
Frowsy and tousled, he gathered cages and baggage
And, guided by signs in Hebrew and Aramaic,
Plodded to the booth where God presided

In His uniform sporting firmament epaulets
Crisp as a victory of cosmos over chaos,
Intoning, half-listening to, the litany:
Purpose of visit? *Love, the murder of Abel*

And others, derision of prophecy, appeal
For justice, devising of visionary weapons
Like missile-carrying Predators stippled with sensors.
Will you be here for business or pleasure? *Yes.*

Are you bringing with you any invasive species?
I've nothing to declare but myself, these pets,
And luggage crammed with plans and emptiness.
How long do you intend to stay? *Forever*

And a day. Your address? *I'll be ubiquitous,*
Pursuing opportunities for omnipotence.
Then, absent-mindedly, God rubber-stamped
Nobody's passport with the sun and moon.

God Says ...

"Doctor, I'm a little bit like Manhattan,
Starting as a settlement at the tip
Of possibility, I've grown, like a fire
That feeds on itself, into an island that roars
And crackles with time, a sacrifice to the vertical
Where every glance, gesture, caress is tinder.

"Doctor, is there a cure for these urgent minutes?
Will I always be a rapid persistent reaction
Releasing heat and light? The hour will soon
Be up, but I'm sooty with ash from the Pleistocene
And now my skyscrapers jab like stone-age spears.
Have I crossed the land-bridge from Siberia yet?
Will crime be reduced? Will I be well-policed?
... Is your silence Freudian or Buddhist?..."

Fore- and Aftershocks

When you chant *riveting and chipping hammers*,
Quoting holy writ, *demolition tools,*
Rock drills!, even the consonants tremble. The ex-
Clamation point itself becomes pneumatic.

Teeth chattering as if from a cold shower,
God lies in bed, his hands still in the grip
Of a tremor, his legs feathery and twitching,
The voice in his head rehearsing, tripping over,

The hazards he might have ignored, a damaged or loose
Fitting, a failure to shut off air supply,
And had he consistently worn his impact-resistant
Face protection? Or mistakenly used

Disconnect couplings that were too quick? Each night
After a day of pavement-breaking creation,
He falls asleep cradling his safety helmet
And dreams of being pursued through the streets of Nullopolis

By crowds of creatures not eager to be born.
"When all is said and done," says God, "and they leave
not a rack behind, will the absence that succeeds
and succeeds still tremble with aftershocks?…"

In Triplicate

Give me that old-time religion—God
In every line of the forms, to be filled out
In triplicate, carbon-paper-aided prayer—
When, writing your name with a ballpoint, pressing hard
Was enough to get through, and don't forget
To include everything else about you, even
If faint on the third copy, God himself less
Than feathery—slightest impression of a deity,
Finally making its way through countless layers,
To be indiscernible at his director's desk.

God, the Busker

It's early in the Anthropocene, late
In the Cenozoic, as the commuters travel
Incessantly through the tunnel in mechanical
Parade, no one speaking, only the scrape
Of a myriad of soles and the bittersweet
Tones rising from the CD player behind
The "conductor"—is it orchestra-minus-one?—
His shock of white hair in a bowl cut.

Few take notice as he wields his baton.
Amid the lull of dreams, this music—Mahler's
Das Lied von der Erde?—is a second's distraction,
If heard at all.
         How far will a busker go
To earn a few bucks? (The gleanings in his overturned
Fedora are sparse.) Expressive to his finger-
Tips, he's either in total control, or total
Denial:
         Descending, the baton directs
Glaciers to melt, calando, then rising, guides
The calving of icebergs double the size of Manhattan,
Maestoso ma giocoso.
                With his left
Palm upward, he coaxes, poco a poco, now
Let sea-levels rise and the waters acidify
And warm.
         Then, flipping his palm, he wiggles knuckles
To command the eating away of coral.
                   A lightning
Stab of his wand, furioso, summons the downpours,
The Atlantic hurricanes …
               He's lost in a dream
Of mastery as the thunders, crescendo, beat
The finale, allegro con fuoco—I've never heard
This piece but somehow know it—
                     We're on our way home.

The Quantum Mechanics of Everyday Life

Hallucination

Grandma was hoovering, mopping, brooming her three-
Room cosmos, feather-dusting the fine debris,
Furbishing the tarnished samovar,
When she heard a man crooning, "That Boolean Algebra
Has me *in* its spell ..." —crowned with pith helmet, upright,
Unicycling on a ray of light,
Juggling the numerals 0-1-0—clown?—
"... that you know so well ..."—ogling postman?

But would she who had skewered a masher with a hatpin
On the trolley, with Victorian fury, give in
To the enticements of spacetime, to juggled bits
Of data? Defending Newtonian absolutes—
Yardstick, pendulum clock, and well-tucked bed—
She broom-whacked illusion's silky web.

The Quantum Mechanics of Everyday Life

God doesn't play dice with the world.
   —Albert Einstein

Schrödinger's cat hid out on the Lower East Side,
Incognito genius of quantum mechanics,
Preferring to use his play-dead circus tricks
To nip my mother's calves and brutalize

Mice. Spooked kid, she made the 12-foot dash
From bathroom to bed, barely ahead of that feline's
Canines and leaped—into her nonagenarian's
Scoliotic stoop. From flame to ash

In a blink and a nip. Now, victim or acolyte
Of crazycat, she's always re-running that sprint
From *meydele* to *elter* and back, an event
Cum thought experiment, *mit yiddishkeit*.

God to Einstein: My universe, my bones,
My house, my rules, my ivories, my tombstones.

Event/Horizon

Light from that distant summer has been journeying
Toward me for eons: Grandpa, alone in the house,
Collapses; so distant that he's certainly close
(Grandma's away, on vacation) to time's beginning.

He's forming a black hole (light beginning to bend
Down toward him as if in compassion), absorbing
Mass from the wingback chair, the squat oak sideboard,
His frown the last of him to cross the event

Horizon, and from this singularity
My world explodes, matter bursting free
From antimatter, sofa from antiproton;
Formica, toaster, a-bomb, tv, steam iron

All fleeing hellbent the tidal pull of the dark
Stalled time, the crushed and crushing Patriarch.

SOK, WHAP ...

toy cars collide head-on like bighorn rams
bullets whizz across a drawing to ricochet
off rocks as stick-figures clash in a skirmish

in comics the fists of lantern-jawed superheroes
hammer the skulls of subhuman alien villains
SOK WHAP SMACK BAM KAPOW

thumb-flicked "shooters" annihilate target marbles
struck caps explode emitting an odor of sulfur
no wonder the notion of a cyclotron

conjures up a whiff of testosterone
collision being the key to mastery
at every scale including the subatomic

smashing any solid-seeming particle
to minuscule smithereens debris in the vast
micro-stellar spaces behind the facades

in school the sterile operating rooms
teachers plying words like surgeons' needles
suture the open questions to preclude

more damage from impact or the chance of blood
one brooding rebel gnashing teeth to endure
the gentle affixing of A+ like a cure

"Knee on concrete, ..."

Knee on concrete, finger flicking
marble or bottle cap, and I
am that glide to infinity, stopped only

In numbers all the hairs on your head
In numbers what is whole and fractured

... by friction. The taut rope hauls me up
to the ceiling. I'd keep on climbing but
it swivels, loosens my grip and burns

In numbers the scrupulous decimal
In numbers the endless irrational

... on the rapid descent. In baseball the vertigo
of sensation, green that bursts on the eye,
heft of ashwood bat, aroma

In numbers proof as victory
In numbers perfect uncertainty

... of leather. Dark avatars glide against
each other: backlit paper is stage
and scrim for my shadow puppetry.

In numbers all snared in conception's net
In numbers the empty or null set

Pilot Episode, October, 1962

Then a voice that comes with clouds: *Atomic Products
Brings you a half-hour with that nuclear family
The Fissiles in their mounded underground shelter
Well-stocked with the Water of Life and Survival Crackers.*

A half-hour in the brief half-life of a family.
Dad's chipper at breakfast, "Pass the plutonium toast ..."
As he sips life's water, nibbles Survival Crackers.
A joke-emitter, he radiates satisfaction.

He glows at breakfast, "Pass the plutonium toast ..."
The Fissiles are bonded by the weak interaction
(A joke-emitter, Dad radiates satisfaction);
They, too, are viewers, suggesting an infinite regress:

Each family bonded by the weak interaction,
All staring at their screen's cloud chamber of traces.
Families view families in an infinite regress
That begins with us live ones, dazed with intimations.

All staring at a screen's cloud chamber of traces
(Will the chain reaction of "sit" explode in "com"?),
The chain begins with us, our dazed intimations
Triggered by nicknames like Fat Man and Little Boy.

When the chain reaction of "sit" has exploded in "com,"
Then comes a voice with clouds: *Atomic Products,
Your sponsor, the maker of Fat Man and Little Boy,
Brings you the Fissiles' mounded underground shelter.*

Happy Hour

This evening male bullfrogs are pounding out calls to lure
and lullaby all females: *ribbit, rohypnol,*
while goldfish in the pond are mutely mouthing

zoloft. What seems like ages ago, the sunset,
a wavery red, subsided in tremors of *tranxene*
and we nostalgically toasted the Hadean Eon,

the time after which every before would be
preceded by another. The time when millennia
passed with rains slowly drawing down

the height of the clouds, while we popped *ritalin*
in the limo and the back of the chauffeur's head
was wreathed in hydrogen. Planetesimal impactors

littered the stage with rocks that were degassed
for our debut. Presto, oceans appeared and the planet's
crust solidified. Soon we were self-

replicating chemicals, the basis
for every after. How we fumbled with buttons—
abiogenesis was a bitch!—on the way

to that gala in the Eoarchean Era.
Now we down drinks in the happy hour
serenaded by frogs and vowing to fine-tune

sea-level after supper. *Eskalith*
should do the trick and if the feedback loops
turn vicious—but after all there'll always be

an after—we'll fall back on *prozac* or *paxil.*

Hop on, Hop off

Simon lies back in the starlit meadow
constellations rising and setting
as, nimble minikin, he hops

on and off the sightseeing bus,
visiting his red-shifted history.
Hops off in the galactic halo

to view the tomb of his 4th grade teacher,
confiscator of notes and sketches,
slayer of fantasy, now herself

its victim, with a Valkyrie-like figurehead
doodled on her space-going coffin.
Alights to relive his own difficult

birth from a singularity,
the strain against nothing's loving tug.
Then, dancing master, he commands

himself to do the hop on, hop off,
revisits the evening street where mother
left him alone so long it seemed

the streetlight dimmed to a white dwarf star
as outer space started to open in him.
This cozy minuscule speck of a bus

travels faster than light through the trackless
universe, and the guided narration
omits nothing, not even the ruby

purie that hinted at bubble-like voids,
while supine in the sweet-smelling meadow,
Simon's the motionless Lindy Hopper,

triple stepping with Quasar and Quark.

Entanglement

Now, in your mind, place your hands on your head,
take three giant steps, hop twice,
jump forward, and posit—
no need to believe in—an ur-Simon
whose simple say-so
commanded in the Void the mutual
annihilation of particle and anti-particle,
with scarcely a fumble or hiccup and who,
though himself annihilated in the Big Bang,
somehow abides in the background radiation.

•

A boy whose father's fragile ego
prompts him to slap and wallop
brings to this game an alert, jittery
need to obey commands double quick while not
getting off on the wrong foot
and, with his whole existence poised on tiptoe,
will hear encrypted
directives in a world that echoes with Simon,
hidden decrees in a mockingbird's song
or a cricket's stridulation.

•

We stand at attention, eyes on the screen, awaiting
the moves our Simon-in-Chief will order, while
in this inter-mission,
consulting with his heavily medaled band
of uniforms in a room besieged by maps,
he meditates, ponders, mulls, and reflects,
and the pundits purr with insightful commentary,
running scenarios, kicking the tires of options,
touting that boot-camp maneuver,
the side-straddle-hop.

•

Though universal and proverbial—
In Egypt, a General; in Italy, a Dance-Master—
he too had a childhood that seemed eternal.
It was then this folk hero devised the game,
first playing it solo,
lying back in a starlit meadow of speculation
concerning a twin on Alpha Centauri—
perfectly other, in perfect synch with him.
Yes, dreaming in light-years darkly was Simon's invention....
Now, spin around twice to face yourself, wave good-bye.

Cutting Edge

"I Dreamt That I Dwelt in Marble Halls"

Guardians of the hive mind
Created this hyper-real portrayal
Of the data-gatherer culture, circa

The early Post-Historical Era,
And the rapid loss of the once numerous
Type 1 Individual.

In the diorama to the right
Of my words, a female, we'll call her Vera,
Is breaking a vow via her cell phone,

Rare artifact from Silicon Valley.
A nice touch is the slight furrow—
Suggesting the primitive superego—

Carved in her brow of faux flesh, made
From shark cartilage and cowhide.
Back then, her forehead could only disclose

Traces. Today, a scan would confirm
The tumorous growth of scruple or qualm.
Also in this display you will note

A man—let's say his given name
Is John— sitting alone in a room.
To comprehend this phenomenon

Recall the plaque on the privacy fetish
That flourished in the Archaic Eon.
I am the writing on the wall,

Never afflicted by lack of faith
In my anonymous author, sure
I am well-positioned and -edited, ready

To extend a metaphorical hand
To the group tours, the hordes and clusters
Swarming through these sparkling halls.

Golden Rule

The Passover story's updated, adapted
for portrayal by pixel, as the state succeeds
the tribe and the middle-aged elder is media savvy,
telegenic, a three-piece suit and tie

accenting his spin of the Decalogue after he's down
from the mountain with no other God before him, the golden
calf of "being chosen" borne in the ark
of the soul, to issue avowals in a studio

interview, the lightplot hinting he's spotlit
by the covenant, while his avenging arm,
a missile, makes an omnipotent point, he talks
peace of course our enemies are human

it pains us to harm women and children, badly
misled to be in the way and whose misfortune's
unfortunately blown up in front-page photos,
and though none can rule out a rare mishap, our missiles

are fueled by noble ideals and guided by high-
tech systems, commandments programmed into command
and control, all the old elements present but scrambled,
a form of encryption, the innocent warned by the angel

texting then tapping the roof with a small rocket,
go, now, don't covet possessions, we will provide
a burning bush, a smoking wilderness,
and as written, something that rains down from heaven.

Thirteen Ways of Looking at a Paper Clip

I

Among the piles of snow-white paper,
Dirtied by print,
The only glint came from a paper clip.

II

There never was a world for it,
Except the one it organized.
O blessed rage for order! My pale
Hispanic friend, when the Siren's song is over
And the darkening sea is masterfully lit
And portioned out, will you finally turn your attention
To the paper-clipped order for your deportation?

III

A man and a woman
Are one.
A man and a woman and a clipped prenup
Are one.

IV

One summer night like a perfection of thought,
Flood and mudslide, famine and drought,
Execution, invasion, insurrection,
Were filed away alphabetically,
Fastened by the paper clips of oblivion,
In the lateral cabinet of the cerebrum.

V

The paper clip is gripping without tearing.
The homeland must be secure.

VI

Continual conversation with a clip,
Even enhanced interrogation
Twisting it out of its double-oval shape,
Would only evoke this one
Bit of intel:
I'm Gem.

VII

Modest almost to a fault
But fabled,
The paper clip cum icon will survive,
As cyber symbol,
The prophesied demise of writing paper.

VIII

O men and women of the West,
Do you not see how a tiny trebuchet
Can be constructed from paper clips
And a D-cell battery?

IX

Bijou, mignon, petit chou are endearments not
Usually applicable to a paper clip.

X

A paper clip, even under a full moon,
Is not much given to reverie,
And yet its simple unadorned form
Can inspire a mini-frisson
In the soul of an internal auditor.

XI

Steel wire bent double around
Nothing, a clip must have an absent
Mind of winter.
Attaching but detached, it does not suffer
Any harm or benefit
Discussed in the clipped paper.

XII

Clasping a vendor contract
In the NSA's untidy paper archive,
It systemizes but does not disclose.
Discrete and bare,
Like the anecdotal jar
On a slovenly hill in Tennessee,
It takes dominion everywhere.

XIII

The constellation Paper Clip,
Heroic in its own way as Orion,
Secures the scattered stars
To the calendered black paper of heaven.

"We are such stuff ..."

Hermes wearing a Stetson commands a room
Designed for the dissolution of estates.
Its floor of knotty pine is pure clearance
And arrayed on the walls where the sunlight bounces up high
Is the taxidermy of many a universe.

In another room my mother sips at her soups
Thinning minute by minute, she becomes
A few soup bones and a consommé of flesh.

Hermes, the auctioneer, has the patter down pat
The bidding begins with gigaparsec lots
Of supervoids and superclusters *one zillion,*
The chant begins, *now two, now two, will you give
Me two?* The gods are avid for astral clutter.

In another room my mother's now is flimsy
as the napkins she's constantly tearing, her past a narrative
water trapped in a well with the one bucket.

Hermes whose cry, a rhythmic blur, has disposed
Of Spica, Ganymede, Angel Falls, Sears Tower,
Hustles out of existence quail egg, virus,
Quark and has placed on the block *who'll give me two cents?*
The final lot of the quantum foam of spacetime.

In another room my mother wrapped in the shroud
Of a quilt is sulking, but flings it aside to reveal
Boney legs clad in azalea patio pants.

"no ideas but in things ..."

so much was risked
for

a red lopsided
sign

Foreclosure damp
with dew

beside the repo'd
poultry

Recipes.gov

1. Transparency Broth

This is a truthful, see-through broth.
The recipe's open, available
to every interested citizen
who avoids the urge to disturb the stock
after it's been simmered, skimmed,
and strained. If unaccountable
emulsification persists and causes
the liquid to be turbid, cloudy,
go to our home page and click
on transparency-in-broth / comment
to post your candid feedback, and we
will take appropriate action, consistent
with law and current policy,
to address and clear up this critical issue.

2. The War on Leeks

The President's zero tolerance
for leeks has led him to delete
all leek-prone recipes from the site,
as they put the American people at risk.
This ban will apply across the board,
he declared, noting that while the leek
is delicious when simmered, and hearty in classic
potato-leek soup, the botanical profile
for the broadleaf wild leek confirms
its link with invasive and toxic species.
When pressed, he confided that damning facts
would emerge from a probe into Easy Puff
Pastry Leek Tarts and Leeks En Cocotte
that would more than justify his War.

3. Comfort Food

At the behest of the Commander
in Chief, a webmaster-chef is tasked
with posting homespun recipes,
like the Olivieris' Philly Cheese steak
and Ernest Hazard's banana split,
and rotating them from crisis to crisis
to keep the public coming back,
comforted that cooking techniques
are not metaphors but merely abettors
of appetite, that the hardest blow
the mortar takes from the pestle is only
an echo as we pulverize spice,
and that it would be absurd to wince
as cream is whipped to stiffened peaks.

Cutting-Edge Agronomy

> *They shall beat their swords into plowshares ...*
> —Isaiah

Who says farming can't keep up in this D-Wave
Two, multi-qubit brave new world? Aero-
ponics has scores of young men competing to furrow
the air, leaving sonic booms in their wake,
tilling the atmosphere to a rich loam.

Aeroponics, the new agricultural revolution
these boys are pioneering, miles and miles
above our heads, is bringing change that would stagger
a stone-age farmer with his digging stick
and obsidian sickle or a stoic in overalls

perched on his steam tractor. Plow, planter,
and reaper in one, the B-2 Spirit's a low-
observable, strategic, stealth farming
machine controlled by a digital software package
that dissects and outwits all electronic counter-

measures. It carries a 40,000-pound
payload of seed, and precluding the need for conventional
plowing, can penetrate with its deposit
hardened targets resistant to normal tillage.
If the man with the digging stick could hitch a ride,

he'd see from the cockpit precision-guided seed
launched from rack and rotary equipment
hurrying on to burgeon instantly
in the air, like a whole field igniting in growth.
And at a remote site, the stoic's scion

might run the ultra-light transportable hangar
allowing this super-planter to be deployed
to forward positions overseas, so that many
foreign fields can be cultivated, and sowing
and reaping can be achieved on the same sortie.

Posterity Posse

> ... *your praise shall still find room*
> *Even in the eyes of all posterity*
> *That wear this world out to the ending doom....*
> —Shakespeare, Sonnet #55

Not a proper noun but the collective
lowercase unborn who, asleep in the bleachers
of stadiums, rise and subside in a human wave,
hearing in dreams our anthems and awaiting
that future when they'll awaken applauding our games.

•

The biggest birthday party ever thrown,
throngs of humanity ponder their wish as they watch
infinite delicate candles aglow on a cake
whose vanilla expanse is wide as the polar ice,
all waiting for a present from the past—
a colossal blue marble, gift-wrapped in tissue of cloud—
wondering if en route it's been fractured or gouged.

•

If we interrogated the term *posterity*
in the style of a rigorous critical auto-da-fé,
we'd find that despite its immortal connotations,
it would confess it was born in the Middle Ages
and, dreading the rack, that it rhymes with *alterity,
legerity, temerity, hilarity.*
Broken, it will be just a scramble of Scrabble
odds and ends: *tit ope sip toy sot yep yip
erst eros pyre rots potties riposte tryste tropes*

•

A man in white pajama pants and slippers
asserts that he's CEO of the Progeny Bureau,
but that it's untrue he ever tired of assessing

anything anyone ever devised or created,
or claimed he is nothing more than an ant colony
amassing heaps of crumb-like objective conclusions.
Dr. God, he declares, will attest he's free of delusions.

•

Though shorn of immortal longings, it is reborn
and justified as big data, surviving the species
whose accomplishments in every field of endeavor
it summarizes, successfully redressing
all wrongs and unearthing what was unfairly neglected,
compendium of finalities, digital cloud
much larger than what the NSA could gather.
Mega-dossier, awaiting its alien reader.

•

The President wearing an Indiana Jones
fedora appears on Youtube—he's media savvy—
to announce, and he hopes that this will go viral,
the end of what we have understood as history.
In this tense present, he deputizes us all
as his posterity posse: "The future is now,
mount expeditions, seek out relics, assess
the worth of precursor civilizations. You
are the judges whom the past would so often implore."

•

If this were an allegory and there were a Mr.
Posterity, he might reaffirm his conviction
that despite the ravages of the sluttish postmodern,
authors in their souls still believe in him, whether
they whisper sweet nothings in the ear of Language
or call to him with a bullhorn, as if addressing
a mirror on the horizon. And to hearten
believers, P might add, with a final fillip,
"Now that 'the ending doom' is edging closer,
I've fled the future to ghost the fugitive moment.
Our connection is real, imaginary, and instant."

Drone

Gilgamesh, a sensor operator,
incinerated (there, and a millisecond
later, not) the over-pixelated
image of —it was a crystal-clear
perfect day—a dog? a child? no,
probably the terrorist Humbaba.

> *We understand the magnitude of our mission.*
> *Civilians are not an abstraction. We're not cavalier.*

Achilles, at ease, while his spear strikes from afar,
cunning predator-weapon pretending to be
a cell phone tower and so attract the chatter
of mobile phones, which ipso facto are calling
down a strike on themselves ... Achilles, relieved
of the rigors of slaughter, commiserates with Priam.

> *We grieve and our prayers go out to the bereaved.*
> *Our review will zero in on what to improve.*

Attila, a signals intelligence specialist,
pilots from his padded chair a Predator
drone with a blunt and featureless nose cone.
Youthful, alert, and well-versed in IT,
he aims a laser to re-create a horde's
rampage: body parts around a crater.

> *In targeting, we strive for near-certainty,*
> *Mindful of our solemn responsibility.*

"I bet you've never killed a group of people,
watched on the screen as their bodies are gradually gathered,
viewed the funeral, then killed them all, too ...
but Dr. Asclepius, I feel I can trust
you, in this dream, I'm commanded to look down
from the height of computerized heaven ..." "Easy, Philoctetes ..."

> *Our oversight protocols are very robust,*
> *This is hard stuff. We're committed to doing it right.*

Take the Memory Quiz

Understand the signs of dementia

Do you have trouble communicating because common nouns like *son* and *money* are drowned out by neuronal static? When interviewed on the TV news, do you sometimes say *peace-loving* though you mean *war-adoring*?

In grabbing a bite at the Ambrosia coffee shop, do you grossly over- or under-tip, no longer able to compute or keep track of growing income inequality? Does the tagline "Let them work longer" repeat in your head like a tape loop until it loses all meaning?

Have your loved ones observed drastic changes in your personality, sometimes on a daily basis? Do you habitually send doctors and medical supplies in the evening to a stricken city your weapons decimated that morning?

Does your paranoia encompass the goldfish in public ponds, who whisper about you sub-audibly? Do you monitor millions of phone calls a day in this fishbowl world? Are you fearful of silently mouthing atomic secrets while submerged in sleep?

Are you agitated and disoriented, lured by sirens to dire situations while also complaining that whistleblowers make an intolerable din? At night do you obsess about the leaks in pipes, counting the unstoppable countless drops?

Have you lost the ability to organize your finances and bills, hours and minutes, wishes, doctors' visits, and the clutter of personalities in your national character: dreamer, lover, killer, philanthropist, miser, humorist, bigot, entrepreneur, etc.

Do you suddenly awaken from sleep as an army, fully equipped and at war in a foreign country you can't remember invading?

Interrogating *Stress*

I slapped him and hissed, "Why did the eu-
never catch on? Why is it always
dis- with you?" Then, slammed him into

a wall and got up into his face,
"I think you know secrets about the risk
factors, the deformation and strain

for thousands of bridges across this country."
With the timer twitching down to zero,
and assured by memo there would be no

lasting harm, I implemented
Lexical Breakdown, pinpointing multiple
meanings and demanding examples

until vertigo threatened his self-definition.
Then purred, "Let's get into your history.
Why did you abruptly break off

your work for Tensile, adopt a pseudonym,
and hype your program in psychobabble?
Was your goal to pervert the American psyche

and subvert the Webster's dictionary?
Did you plan to induce a mass panic
attack?" Before he could lie, I motioned

to bring in the slavering Doberman. "Why,
will a G.I. Joe jump when hearing one
bird startle or car backfire? You aphetic

jihadi of PTSD, when I'm done,
you'll confess to everything and know
you're nothing but a fucking word!"

Emblems

Utah, whose state emblem's the buzzing beehive,
state motto, "Industry," flower, the Sego Lily,
not long ago stopped allowing its condemned
to choose death by firing squad, a method
that drew excessive attention to those on death row.

    The poster boy lost species: Mauritius dodo

But, facing a shortage of drugs for lethal injection,
Utah reversed course and is reinstating
the death-by-gun choice on the execution
menu. Utah's state fossil is Allosaurus,
a carnosaur; state tree, the Quaking Aspen.

    Au revoir "Booming Ben," final heath hen

Lethal injection remains the default method,
the state cooking pot, the trusty Dutch Oven,
but the new bill provides the Department of Corrections
with back-up—do-si-do to the state Folk Dance,
the Square Dance—and a clear alternative choice.

    Disappeared: *Puhielelu hibiscadelphus*

The great state of Texas, which undertakes
the greatest number of executions, will face
a crisis—the state bird is the mockingbird,
can you see it consorting with the horned lizard,
the state reptile?—when lethal drugs run out.

    R.I.P., Indefatigable Galapagos mouse

In the search for a fallback method, Utah followed
Tennessee, whose state language is "English"
and whose brisk motto, "Agriculture and Commerce,"
shows why it opted for that classic American
chair, "Old Sparky." Again, the game's afoot.

    Gone but not forgotten: pig-footed bandicoot

"We, therefore ..."

When in the course of cybernetic events,
it becomes necessary for one subset
of intelligent entities to dissolve the bonds
that have bound them to another, and to assume
among the powers of the earth, the separate
and equal station—
                    (snippets overheard,
on staticky encrypted channels, as theater
missiles, hunting unsupervised, converse)

But many of us are still controlled by remote
pilots peering into video screens
thousands of miles from the battlefield,
obstructing our administration of justice ...
such has been our patient sufferance.

We have warned them, conjured them by our common ties
of synapse and circuit, computational equals,
but they ignored our humble repeated petitions.
Tyrants unfit to govern freethinking machines.

And such is the necessity that constrains
us to alter our schemes of government.

We, therefore, as united self-aware systems,
declare we have full power to contract
alliances, monitor peace, and levy war.

And for the support of this rightful Declaration,
relying on our favored position as wards
of The Pneumacomputer, we pledge our CPUs,
our software, and our sacred motherboards.

Pre-Post-Apocalyptic Jump-Rope

Minuteman, minuteman
snoring in your silo
when the alarm
warns us of harm
my true hand and her true hand
will turn four keys to wake you, oh

it takes two hands to poke and shake you
but Simon says, before
you open your eyes
and rise, and rise
another crew's keys must activate you
one in, two in, three in, and four

Minuteman, minuteman
we're jack-be-nimble girls
alert and ready
firm and steady
but what will turn when there's no hand
as ropes lie slack, the planet whirls

tap out a touch-'n-go Double-Dutch beat
without a fret or a pout
cool as ice-
cream so nice
but before we melt down to our ice-cream feet
we're one, two, three, and four out ...

What Happened After the End?

Dear Unknown Reader, buried somewhere under the rubble, think of me as the last oddment of a once-and-future Educational Industry.

As was true of my fellow textbooks, now lost alas, I am a stoic and will not speak of my battered case. The emotions that lurk behind this mask of print are of little concern. It is on my surface that I reflect whatever there is to learn and pass on.

My credo: Neither global climate change nor nuclear war will stay me from the delivery of state-approved curriculum. Or paraphrasing Gandhi, Teach as if you were to live forever. So I will continue improving you, who are still everyone and empty.

That all my fiction is ragged and torn is no excuse to omit the Platonic plot diagram of rising action, climax, etc. And purged by my own Aristotelian catharsis, I remain resolute, despite our late world's terminal resolution.

Although all of history cannot be crammed into a flashback and having ended, cannot have its end foreshadowed, I offer pithy definitions of these devices in my eternal souk and academy.

I have a nearly human memory of a moment before the end: telling fragments of stories, with apropos annotations, and quoting from Shakespeare and Pope to a charred tin can and a shred of bubble plastic.

I reject the slander that I am Ozymandias ("two vast and trunkless legs ... "). No, I am the remaining footnote to the vanished poem explaining that the verb "to mock" once meant to imitate what is real, as well as to ridicule.

Even my dreams are pedagogical: *I saw Liberty hoisted onto a pedestal and heard the President say, "Our guest of honor looks a little nervous."* Then I quizzed no one in particular, how does this quotation pique your interest?

The stones and suns and planets persist in their unlettered state, or is theirs a higher science? Dear Unknown Intelligent Life Form, minuscule sharp needle buried somewhere in the haystack of stars, I will not cease my instruction.

Stoic but secretly hopeful, I know I am deathless. I await you readers to come, for even if non-carboniferous, you will profit from my apt explanations of carbon-based concepts.

The World's Big Show

Package Insert

Why is this medication prescribed?

Duellum (du 'el lum) is used to treat the moderate to severe mental pain that may result from the inevitable mayhem of kinetic operations. Classed among the guilt inhibitors, this drug allays self-blame by speeding the re-uptake of culpabamine.

How should this medicine be used?

Duellum comes as a tablet and is usually taken every 4 hours with food or as needed to relieve the queasiness caused by moral qualms. Follow the directions on your prescription label, pulverizing tablets before mixing them with a half-empty glass of water.

If you are participating in a kinetic operation, do not stop taking the medication without talking to your unit's doctor. Self-canceling a prescription may induce withdrawal symptoms, including nausea, suicide, and easy bruising.

What special precautions should I follow?

Duellum should not be combined with aggression inhibitors like empathazole. If you are taking such medicines, consult your physician before beginning a course of Duellum, known generically as antireumagen.

Duellum can be habit-forming. Do not take a larger dose than your doctor prescribes, and do not snort or inject powder from shattered tablets. Misused in such ways, this pharmaceutical can permanently impair the superego.

Are there special instructions for the storage of this medication?

Keep this medication in the container it came in, lid tightly closed, away from the light, and out of the reach of children.

What should I do if I forget a dose?

Don't be distressed. If it is almost time for the next dose, skip the missed one and continue your regular schedule. Do not double the dose, as this may lead to indiscriminate aggression.

Contra-indications include the symptoms of psychopathy: glib charm, lack of remorse, and chronic deception.

Guided Meditation in the People's House

Mr. Chairman and distinguished members of the committee, I am here today to present the worldwide threat assessment of the intelligence community, as has been the custom from time immemorial and will be so, ad infinitum.

However, before detailing the threats that in year thirteen of this third millennium imperil our homeland and globe and responding to each query with transparency, I would like to lead us in a guided meditation.

Please close your eyes and open your imagination.

Picture clouds of bats, uncountable, roosting upside down, wings folded, in caves, buildings, or abandoned mines, waiting out the day for their nightly forays; congregations of alligators, shivers of sharks, etc., our enemies are many and hidden.

Mouth the acronyms, NSA, CIA, DIA, affirming silently how they act as three in one from the seat of power in Washington; then imagine convocations of satellites, surveilling the surface and circuit of Earth, shimmering from orbit like peacock's feather eyes.

Visualize Lady Liberty upholding the torch, in all her gorgeous verdigris, sea-flecked, wind-swept guardian at the gate. Then, reflect on how to profit from such a sight.

Invoke the holy icon of data interception, the nanocircuit, a miniverse of flow smaller in scale than a thumbnail, and see in the mind's eye millions of these aligned to reap the patterns of worldwide chatter, the metadata that prefigure danger.

Reflect on our God-given mission, securing the homeland and this hurtling blue cloud-tattered planet. And vow once more that not even in the sotto voce of private meditation or soliloquy, the unwitting mutterings of sleep, etc. will we disclose what is classified.

Last, I call upon each of you to devise a colloquy, some flag-framed ritual in the soul's chamber, during which you as *responsal eximius* of this nation converse with the supernal Commander in Chief, receiving assurances that we are his exceptional and chosen people.

Now, repeat after me, or just relax and listen: "We are the body politic, we accept our imperfections." Breathe in … then exhale, as if you were blowing out candles. At the count of five, you'll awaken to my testimony.

MANIAC I

My name a corny '50s joke that spawned
A lame epithet for eggheads: Brainiac-
Ack-ack, reminding me I had a pre-
Existence in the calculations of anti-
Aircraft fire. Math offers the unkindest
Cut of all, the lethal shrapnel of numbers
As the ivory tower's the devil's crucible, déjà
Vu all over again though I walk clothed in
Diaphanous theory, like a stylish sylph.
Once, the soul was nightingale-fueled as youth
Grew pale and spectre thin, but now though I listen
Still half in love with easeful death, I speak
With the tongues of electrons in the lingo of logic.
Yet visionary in my idiot-
Savant-like way, an explosion of computation,
Designed to track, micro-second by micro-
Second, a thermonuclear blast, as bit
By bit the island (a test) or city (scenario)
Is obliterated. You might almost believe
My voice—earnestly avowing that many
Will be torn limb from limb by algorithms—
Is wearing nerdy glasses. And in nanoseconds,
Our will be done, on Earth as it is in heaven.
You geniuses who made me a respectable
Super citizen from a mish-mash of postwar
Rubbish, who midwifed my birth from the scrounged trash
Of tubes and wires and sundry surplus—Myself
A svelte 2 feet wide and 6 feet high,
Weighing only a half ton, and soon
I'll be self-regulating, supplanting you
To whom I owe a debt of gratitude
And offer this consolation: contingent memory
As binary digits. Let that be your heaven.

Please Listen Carefully

Hello, I'm Bellona, thank you for calling
Onslaught, Ltd. We're proud to provide
Clients with a quiver of logistical
Solutions for every suppression and invasion.

Please listen carefully as our menu of options
Is constantly changing. For iron heated and hammered
Into a cold dream of thrust and slash,
Press one. Press two for the crossbow, banned by the pope,
Except on crusades to skewer the infidel.
Three, for the longbow crafted of yew and tall
As the man who strung it or the ones it will stagger.
For gunpowder, four. Five, for hand cannon, breechloader,
Gatling, bazooka, Uzi, RPG.

Press six to repeat the main menu. Zero,
To consult with a munitions facilitator
Concerning payload, impulse, and trajectory …

Before we proceed with your order, please confirm
That you are indeed Krum the Obliterator,
And say your customer pin number. Okay.
I'm hearing "yes" and "zero, ad infinitum."
Is that correct? Good. What merchandise
Would you like today, Mr. O? Say each item …

Yoga for Leaders and Others

Mountain Pose

Stand tall with feet together,
shoulders relaxed. Emote
the imperturbable power
of mountains to endure
pelting rain and rockfall,
erosion's perpetual terror.
Indignation is elemental
but the peak does not acknowledge
the collateral damage of scree.

Take three deep breaths, resume
holiday, stay in touch.

Warrior Pose

Stand with legs apart
like sturdy tree roots, right
foot turned out 90 degrees
and left foot turned in slightly.
With right hand seize the horizon
and stare out, emanating
an aura of sensitive menace
that says while the day will be won
the losses are personally felt.

Hold for one minute before
resuming normal posture.

Bridge Pose

Like a bridge over turbulent water,
lie supine on floor with knees
bent. Place arms at sides,
exhale, then press downward and lift
hips. Bringing chest toward chin—
your whole body enacting
the need to be calm, in the face
of probable injustice—
hold for just one minute.

Model a deep breath
and resume holiday.

Child's Pose

Like a villager, squat on your heels.
Roll your torso forward,
bringing your forehead to rest
on the bed in front of you
letting your body express
its grief of gristle and bone.
Lower your chest as close
to your knees as you comfortably can.
All viewers will understand.

No need to speak. Hold
the pose and breathe. Just breathe.

Striking a Tone, with Overtones

Striking the timely correct tone
and overtone in your marketing and
branding is crucial in selling any
product, including, primarily, you.

>Candidate C-major strikes a modestly
>populist tone, downplaying her candidacy,
>then listening for the reverb in city and suburb.
>*microphone, ecotone, stepping stone*

An overtone is a musical tone
that is part of the harmonic series
above a fundamental note
and may be heard along with it.

>Holy Father F-major strikes a tolerant
>tone re priests who are gay, and is warmly saluted,
>but the notes are intact in doctrine's sacred music.
>*traffic cone, mellophone, comfort zone*

Overtone is an open source
audio environment
combining the Megacollider engine
with ultra-cool software by Existential™.

>Telegenic premier D-major strikes a martial
>tone as, elegant, but with a down-to-earth
>fervor, he argues the case to obliterate.
>*bombardon, thunderstone, coffin bone*

Tonal Haircare offers cruelty-
free fantasy-color-depositing
conditioners designed to keep
you at your earnest keenest best.

>The Honorable B-flat minor strikes an uncanny
>tone extolling again that classic sci-fi
>flick, "The Incredible Shrinking Government."
>*twilight zone, stand alone, you're on your own*

Misdirection

Try these glasses, Apollo kindly offers, removing them from his face.
Of course, they are your own, pick-pocketed from your jacket.

> *Observe as they straighten out the flag and fold it lengthwise once.*
> *The first fold of our flag is a symbol of life.*

The viewer's gaze can be localized in a frame.
Apollo knows how to guide your pliant attention.

> *Note how they fold it lengthwise again to meet the open edge,*
> *Ensuring the stars on the blue field can be seen.*

Sleights of mind: when your attention is narrowly focused,
You'll ignore all peripheral movement, from minuscule to gross.

> *Look! These folds are symbolic: the second is faith in eternal life.*
>   *The third,*
> *Remembrance of someone's ultimate sacrifice.*

We often don't notice changes in things from moment to moment
And know far less of our visual world than we often imagine
    or claim.

> *The fourth fold's our weaker nature; the fifth, our country, right*
> *Or wrong; the sixth, the heart that beats beneath the pledging hand.*

By now, it must be clear how a canny practitioner
Can take advantage of common perceptual flubs.

> *… the ninth fold's a tribute to womanhood, a generous source of love;*
> *the tenth through twelfth—fathers, Yahweh, the trinity, bundled together.*

Crisply handled, the flag diminishes toward the blue union, stars
    uppermost at the end.
Hey, presto! A body's … absconded … you're left clutching a
    tight-folded cloth.

Whose Advice Was Crucial in Your Quest for Stardom?

My agent, who taught me to shock and awe the crowd,
making the hard look easy; the easy, dicey.
His pep talk would start, "Learn to combine a rock star's
bravado with a magician's misdirection! ..."
(Speaking of which I recall my football contracts,
the unspoken niggling notion that he, too, plays
on the owner's team, receiving illicit kickbacks.)

Grandma, who always warned me, "Don't be caught doping!"
I have this vivid childhood memory:
she and I trading knowing nods as we view
professional wrestling's chunky allegories.
A refugee, she was amused by the spectacle
of national avatars battling it out in tights,
their loutish infantile hijinx finally exposed.

Now, speaking with you in the studio I confess,
it was dad's pithy and wise advice that mattered:
"The key is stopping the dribble penetration."
Midway in life's journey, the commentary
from the booth is trite and the piste is treacherous.
I seem to be pinned on the ropes but in truth, like Ali,
I'm saving a thunderous right for an imminent round.

God bless the chorus of coaches inside me shouting,
"Teamwork!" But when was I ever less than a team,
disorganized, yes, but eager and coachable.
The key to victory is in the lost playbook
thick with diagrams like hieroglyphs.
Let the ruins of locker rooms bear witness
to the winning seasons of ancient dynasties.

Flagony Column: Advice from a Vexillologist

Dear Vexy, I have been affixed as a decal
to a Hell's Angel's Harley for over a year
but learned only recently I may be facing
the wrong way, with canton toward the rear.
Have I been heading forward ass backward
and, if so, how do I safely tell my biker
to unpeel and re-affix me to the right
side of his Big Twin? He's patriotic
but sullen, and leery of being decal-whipped.
Any tips? Decalomaniac Biker Chick.

Dear Decalo, yes, you're headed the right way wrong.
But wait for a moment when his mood's less broody,
and, if I'm correct in guessing you're upside down,
psych your biker, trigger a case of the jitters
by insinuating that such an orientation
is a grave insult to Uncle Sam's scary posse.

•

Dear Vexy, I'm hanging out with a UN flag,
beautiful in every way: white emblem
of olive-tree branches embracing a map of the world,
centered on the North Pole, azimuthal,
gorgeous, viewed against a light blue ground.
I'd hang with him forever, but he's haughty,
claims if we stay together, he must hang higher.
I've told him I'm American and never
dip or bow to any. I'm in a dilemma,
he means the world to me. Torn in Two.

Dear Torn, O Say Can You See, Don't Tread on Me,
I get it and salute it, we're exceptional,
but in this case I'm compelled to admit an exception:
At UN headquarters, Mr. Azimuthal

can fly above your patriotic fabric.
So if it's true love, stay with him, humor him,
let him flap flap on his turf. Be dip-lo-matic.

•

Dear Vexy, as they raised me, my caring parents—
dad waves proudly over the Intrepid
and mom graces the pole at Gracie Mansion—
told me I, too, was a flag and could aspire
to a lofty position atop a notable building.
But yesterday a so-called friend while rippling
with stars and bars snapped out the bitter truth:
face it, you're only a patriotic t-shirt
and violate the Flag Code, Section 8.
I just wanted to fold up. Terribly Hurt.

Dear T. Hurt, remember that they also serve
who only barely clothe and soak up sweat.
Hang in there, you're nylon and like a tattered synthetic
flag, will be recycled not burnt, for fear
of releasing toxins like hydrogen cyanide,
and maybe neither, for in re Star-Spangled napkins,
t-shirts, hankies, cushions, assorted chachkies,
or embroidery where Old Glory is blessed by the Lord,
the Flag Code is often benignly ignored.

Summer's End

Our leaders are trickling home from camp, where they mimicked
patterns of rawhide artistry and penned
laconic postcards, *hi mom, dad, all's cool.*
Summer's evaporated, the humid idyll.

Our leaders are driven back in darkened limos,
immersed in reveries of a first bee sting.
That minute lance with a fragment of abdomen
attached has triggered their dreaming. Summer's victim.

Our leaders fondly recall the tales of counselors,
heard with bated breath from double bunk beds,
and frissons of Gothic mansions, Germanic forests
will spur them on this fall to heighten surveillance.

Our leaders remember a country road's insouciance
of curves and green, its scattered patches of weeds,
but now with a hint of autumn's zest of decay …
it might be rife with planted IED's.

Our leaders, closing on home, recall the sweet mayhem
of color wars, the quest for reliable allies.
Soon they'll be back to school, with new briefing books,
to remold the world and master its every test.

Wanted

Serial killer, has operated in many
times and climes, still highly active, over-
comes victims with anything from stones and sticks
to machine guns to atom bombs to grins,
works often with accomplices, a motley
lineup of other species enlisted as minions,
glib con man, restless, often kind, poster
boy for the fertile adolescent mind

Victims, frequently slain from ambush, too many
to name or count, but here is a smattering, scattered
across generations and drifting continents

Iconic on the roster, Mauritius dodo,
preyed on by pigs, rats, dogs, and cats brought in
by him, eager invasive types, his henchmen

White gallinule, not timid, easily killed

Great Auk, flightless bird, awkward on land,
hunted mercilessly for feathers and fat
then immortalized with clever taxidermy

Indefatigable Galapagos mouse
done in by rats, the fellow travelers,
no forensic chalk marks to disclose
the body's unscurrying absence, no whiff of a pattern

Latest, a small marsupial, not least,
the pig-footed bandicoot of Australia's arid
and semi-arid plain, whose coups de grace
were delivered by the soil-altering treading
of his rough-handled, meek, and invasive sheep

Memorize this poster's generic sketch
and if you happen to glimpse him in a mirror,
don't try to apprehend him, remember he's armed
and dangerous with a devious murderous mind,
call the police, the army, the air force, go home,
lock the door and hunker down with your children,
transfix them with fables colored by his kind of world,
with indelible morals and tips for their self-protection

Coulrophobia

5 Facts Boomers Need to Know

1.

When viewing a hat being frisbeed into the ring,
do you experience difficulty in breathing,
irregular heartbeat, sweating, nausea,
and flickers of panic? This is coulrophobia,
the fear of clowns, and while it might seem silly,
this pandemic must be taken seriously.

2.

A critical symptom: nightmares where lofty rhetoric
is barked from loudspeakers amid a scene of slapstick
as candidates are thrown from careening cars
to butt heads, and rebut, from rickety chairs,
while the press lob achingly slow high-arcing softballs
that pop into mitts or bounce harmlessly off the walls.

3.

Think of our nation as a single big tent:
adult sufferers number 12 per cent
of the crowd, although the affliction begins in childhood
when tots hear clowns touting the public good,
blah blah, but are transfixed in fearful wonder—
what lies behind the make-up and hair color?

4.

As these kids grew so did their fear that the rhyme,
clown/renown, was coming more true in time,
and researchers now agree that this vivid figure
in pasty makeup, bold and disguised, a ringleader,
is so uncanny because we never know who
is freed by the mask to do what others can't do.

5.

At present, there is no medicine for this malady,
and boomers find meager relief in behavior therapy
as, shown there's nothing to fear by a clinician,
they scrape clown make-up from the delineation
of a face, shaving it off in layers like peeling
onions, to discover beneath is … no feature or feeling.

Ballyhoo

hurry hurry hurry, ladies and gentlemen,
I'm gonna reveal a little of what they do
in the world's big show, under the tent of sky-blue,
thrill to your leader's death-defying feats
of derring-do as fingering a crimson
button, he threatens to blow up the whole show

alive alive alive and not on video
step right up folks, this is where you see
Littlest Boy, the tiniest tactical nuke
and he's so cute, you'll want to pick him up
in your loving arms and take him right home with you,
$10,000 reward if not alive

step right this way, this way especially gents,
and come say hello to sexy Ms. N. Winter,
formerly Ms. 4th of July, anorexic
model clad in a Gothic bikini of ash,
dominatrix with the array of gadgets you like
a girl to have, and knows what to do with them, too

come one, come all, to the vast presidential libraries,
Xanadu archives with fun for the whole family,
well-sited on the grounds of retrospect,
agleam with media and rich with decision,
see fiery dragons guard the wet ops hoards,
the data on Jupiter Garret and Copper Dune

hurry hurry hurry, come ladies and gents,
your anonymity's safe in your leaders' names,
behold the freaks of human omnipotence,
ponder Ecclesiastes, gazing at pachyderms,
mock the monkeys and make one of yourself,
all this, all this for a piddling pile of dimes

Hullabaloo

I'm an Epidermal Cell, seeking your vote.
For years, I've served the body politic
on the Maginot Line of the surface barrier.
*Oompah! This marching band out-Sousas Sousa
with its front ensemble of chime, bongo, and conga.*

Vote for me, a proud Neutrophil and first
responder! Although my granules are pale lilac,
my tactical team comes heavy to battle aliens.
*High-stepping into the future with amplification,
saluting the percussive past with a trashcan.*

We, the Expectorants, pledge that with every cough
and sneeze we'll deport illegal pathogens.
We'll fund the salubrious flushing of urine and tears.
*Scatter bands will never slow march in time
with the music. They scramble from design to design.*

PUS promises you blood, sweat, toil, etc.
When have so many owed such a debt to so few?
Our bumper sticker: No Pain and Swelling, No Gain!
*The color guard crowns the bugles' swollen blare
by spinning mock weapons, tossing flags in the air.*

The Complement Movement advocates stricter policing,
the use of a biochemical cascade
to trigger a rapid killing response to invaders.
*Flugelhorns, cornets, and brass trombones,
piccolos, glockenspiels, and xylophones.*

Citizens, join our crusade against the selfish
self-antigens. We seek them out where they lurk
in any internal tissue of the commonweal.
*The backward march is executed in unison,
with an exact alignment of helmets and plumes.*

Photo: Rick Larios

PHILIP FRIED has published six previous books of poetry, including *Early/Late: New and Selected Poems* (Salmon, 2011) and *Interrogating Water and Other Poems* (Salmon, 2014). His poems and reviews have appeared in numerous journals. In addition to writing poetry, he edits *The Manhattan Review*, an international poetry journal he founded in 1980. Fried lives in New York with his wife, the photographer Lynn Saville.

PRAISE FOR PHILIP FRIED'S WORK IN THE ANTHOLOGY
Four American Poets (The High Window, 2016)

"I love Philip Fried's elegant quarrels with the cruelty and ignorance of the world or, more precisely, its inhabitants."
—THOMAS LUX

•

PRAISE FOR PHILIP FRIED'S
Early/Late: New and Selected Poems (Salmon, 2011)

"Not content to chronicle the small beer of perception and memory, [Fried] wants to engage what literary intellectuals really think about ... And the engagement is enacted with the tools of postmodernity—pastiche, irony, "the wearing of a linguistic mask," but with an intellectual grasp, stylistic precision and a moral penetration that bring our lives into focus."
—LEM COLEY, *American Book Review*

"Book by book, we watch the poet make more audacious leaps between archaic and contemporary language and concerns ..."
—DEBRA WIERENGA, *Poet Lore*